MAR 2 9 2018

W9-CRZ-067

A Girl's Guide

# Fashion on a Budget

Karen M. Smith

ELDORADO INK

**Eldorado Ink**
PO Box 100097
Pittsburgh, PA 15233
www.eldoradoink.com

Produced by OTTN Publishing, Stockton, New Jersey

CPSIA compliance information: Batch#GG2017.
For further information, contact Eldorado Ink at info@eldoradoink.com.

First printing

1 3 5 7 9 8 6 4 2

Library of Congress Cataloging-in-Publication Data

on file at the Library of Congress
ISBN 978-1-61900-105-3 (hc)
ISBN 978-1-61900-113-8 (ebook)

**About the Author:** Karen M. Smith works as a freelance writer and editor and lives on a farm in rural Ohio with her husband, two sons, and a menagerie of horses, llamas, alpacas, cats, and one very big, fluffy, white dog. She currently serves as the fantasy editor for Red Sun magazine and is a published author of romantic and fantasy fiction.

**Photo Credits:** Everett Historical: 6 (bottom); used under license from Shutterstock, Inc.: 1, 4, 7, 9 (top, bottom left), 12, 13, 14, 15, 19, 20, 21, 24, 25, 26, 27, 28, 30, 31, 35, 36, 39, 41, 42, 43, cover; Donna Beeler / Shutterstock.com: 6 (top); emka74 / Shutterstock.com: 9 (bottom right).

*For information about custom editions, special sales, or premiums,*
*please contact our special sales department at info@eldoradoink.com.*

# Table of Contents

# Fashion vs. Style

**A**s girls grow up and their personalities become defined, they begin to develop preferences for style. Most girls from the ages of 10 to 18 don't have the luxury of unlimited spending money to indulge in wide exploration of fashion in order to figure out not only what they like best to wear, but which styles look best on them.

Any girl still dependent upon parents or guardians needs to learn how to make those subtle, yet significant, adjustments that will draw the admiration of her peers without breaking her piggy bank.

This book is for those girls.

## A CENTURY OF EVOLVING FASHION

Before the twentieth century, women achieved a fashionable silhouette by reshaping their bodies using corsets and multiple layers of undergarments. That required a time-consuming process and often a ladies' maid just to get dressed. By the late 1800s, a woman's outfit—not including

her hat—could weigh as much as 25 pounds. Her hat could add another 20 pounds.

Multiple layers of clothing, which dragged on the ground and carried dirt and debris, made navigation of everyday life difficult. Hoops (hoop skirts or cages), bustles, and heavy crinolines were hot and awkward. In the late 1800s, concern grew that tightly laced corsets damaged a woman's internal organs. Women's suffrage, surprisingly, did not help the movement to reduce the impositions of feminine garb. Real progress and change followed a growing appreciation for a woman's natural form in the early 1900s.

During the 1890s, simple, more comfortable dresses became fashionable for women.

With the explosive growth of the middle class in the United States, artistic dress drew a strong following from those women who appreciated the freedom and comfort of more comfortable clothing. Neoclassical trends in architecture and fashion also helped move women's fashion forward, allowing for lighter, less constricting styles. The Roaring Twenties brought the advent of moving pictures and widespread feminine support for more relaxed styles of dress.

A beach official checks the amount of thigh exposed by a young lady's bathing suit, 1922. The hemlines on all women's clothing reached new heights during the 1920s.

During the twentieth century, silhouettes changed from the androgynous flapper dress to the poufy crinoline-lined skirts of the 1950s to the loose, flowing, colorful styles of the hippie

generation in the 1960s and early 1970s. Women learned to merge fashion with comfort and pragmatism. Today, women's clothing follows a more fluid set of guidelines, often related to the activity rather than social dictates and assumptions of morality.

## FASHION VERSUS STYLE

The terms "fashion" and "style" differ in meaning, although the difference can be subtle. "Fashion" concerns what top designers are pushing in their seasonal collections. Designs which best impress critics and self-appointed experts filter down through the layers of retail, from high-end boutiques where a single outfit can easily cost thousands of dollars to the discount department stores that sell in high quantities at cheap prices to the general public. The shopper will see substantial differences in quality between those high-end boutiques and discount stores with regard to fabric, cut, and construction of the garments.

During the late 1960s and early 1970s, women's fashion often featured high boots and short, colorful skirts.

Another concept to remember with regard to popular fashion is that "cheap" and "inexpensive" have different meanings. Cheap indicates poor workmanship and inferior quality of materials. Cheap, trendy items won't last long and will quickly go out of fashion. Inexpensive implies a good value for the price and makes no reference to workmanship or quality of materials.

The term "style" refers to the clothing one wears that fits one's per-sonality and creates one's image, though that image can change by venue

# BEFORE YOU BUY

One task before embarking upon that shopping trip is to look at the fashion magazines, such as *Teen Vogue, J-14, Girls' Life, American Cheerleader,* and *Seventeen,* to see what's in style for girls of similar age. Girls who don't subscribe to any of these magazines can probably find some of them at their local libraries.

A girl who's not really sure of her style preferences may consider a trip just for the purpose of window shopping and trying on outfits. Display windows offer fashion suggestions that may look fabulous on the mannequins, but not so much on the girl herself. Upscale clothiers will have the latest fashions in stock. A girl can try them on, learn what she likes and what looks good on her, and then go to a department store or discount retailer and purchase a (much) less expensive version.

The discount store version won't boast the same quality as an upscale clothing store, but some clever altering can fine tune a garment's fit. For example, if a shirt's sleeves are a little too short, then shortening them further to three-quarter length or even shorter can transform a shirt that otherwise fits into a new addition for warm weather wear. Shorten hems to adjust the length of skirts and slacks. Sometimes moving the buttons on a jacket or shirt just a fraction of an inch will make a garment fit perfectly. An experienced seamstress can insert darts in garments that are too big, or take advantage of seam allowances to ease a tight garment's fit.

Bringing a friend on the shopping trip can add fun as well as another set of eyes to evaluate fashion choices. The friend should have the girl's best interests at heart, be honest in her opinions, and understand what she can and cannot afford.

and over time. A girl's image at school will differ from her image on the volleyball court. Her tastes as a 10-year-old will change as she matures, resulting in a much different image when she is a high school senior preparing for adulthood.

There's more to personal fashion than what designers dictate. The idea is to create a look that suits a girl's personality, her body shape, and her coloring. Good fashion and good style hinge on several factors that contribute to the well-dressed girl.

Every girl should remember that just because a famous designer or a fancy boutique shows off a particular style, it doesn't mean that style will look good on her. A girl should avoid wearing something just because it's "in fashion" if it looks terrible on her.

Fashion magazines have been around for hundreds of years and were initially produced for men's clothing. The first fashion magazine for women was published in 1693.

According to The Most, the top three most popular fashion items for the last 100 years are, in order:
1) Converse sneakers
2) the Chanel 2.55 handbag
3) Tiffany pearls.

# WARDROBE STAPLES

Every young woman's closet should include some core items, known as "wardrobe staples." Fashion experts agree that the feminine wardrobe should contain:

- A dress for special occasions or religious services. Girls, especially those younger than sixteen, often need one nice dress to wear for special occasions that merit dressing up.
- White button-down shirt
- A lightweight, drapey t-shirt
- Black, navy, or gray slacks
- Knee-length skirt in a neutral color
- Blue jeans
- Black dress shoes (white for summer)
- Low-heeled ankle boots
- White, black, or neutral cardigan sweater and one in a bright color
- Pearl necklace and earrings (good quality costume jewelry is okay)
- Diamond or cubic zirconia earrings.

Any missing wardrobe staples should be the first items on the shopping list. This will help you avoid impulse purchases that might blow the budget. Quality is of primary consideration in the purchase of wardrobe staples, because these items will be worn repeatedly. Save "cheap" for those trendy items that aren't expected to last more than a season.

# Fit and Style

ashion that looks good is fashion that fits. Clothing that hangs like a pillowcase or stretches like a tight sausage casing should be discarded from a girl's wardrobe. How a girl looks affects how she feels. Clothes that fit properly can boost a girl's self-confidence, and clothes that fit poorly can do just the opposite.

As girls grow and mature, their bodies go through dramatic changes in shape. These changes often frustrate girls trying to find clothing and shoes that fit for longer than a season. It also frustrates their parents, who often foot the bill for complete wardrobe changes every few months. Parents might be tempted to purchase their daughters' clothing a size too big to allow for "growing room." Girls might not be able to prevent that from happening, but there are techniques that can be employed to help make clothes that are slightly too large fit better.

# BODY SHAPE AND FIT

Before embarking upon a shopping trip for the next season's wardrobe, growing girls should measure themselves, or be measured to get a head start on finding clothing that fits. Proper measurement requires a measuring tape, which can be found at any fabric or craft store.

Fitting clothes to a very young girl's body poses little challenge beyond making sure of the correct size—until puberty hits. The development of curves complicates matters. Most girls mature into one of two basic shapes:

**Pear-shaped:** On a pear-shaped body, a girl's hips are the widest part of her body and her shoulders are often one of her best features. The fashion goal with a pear-shaped body is to elongate the figure to de-emphasize the hips and accentuate the top half. Pear-shaped bodies look best in clean, tailored lines with dark colors below the waist and attention getting tops. Even out the silhouette with pants or jeans that have flared legs. Jackets help add substance to the upper body. Different necklines draw attention to the upper body.

**Apple-shaped:** An apple-shaped body tends to be fuller around the middle with broad arms and shoulders. The fashion goal with an apple-shaped body is to de-emphasize the waistline. Girls with apple-shaped bodies look best in small, subtle patterns or solid colors. They often have great legs and larger bosoms and can take advantage of short shirts and tops that pop, drawing attention away from thicker waists. They look best in longer jackets and drop-waist dresses.

Bear in mind that these shapes are general descriptions. Feminine shapes come in an infinite variety. They are affected by the size and shape of other body parts, particularly those who are either short-waisted or long-waisted.

## TAKING MEASUREMENTS

In order to determine size, especially if ordering clothing online, it's important to have accurate measurements. Clothing measurements are taken at specific places on the body, as follows:

**Chest:** Measure the circumference of the chest at the fullest part of the bust.

**Waist:** Measure the circumference of the body at the natural waistline (just above the hips).

**Hips:** Measure the circumference, ensuring that the measuring tape circles around the fullest part of the buttocks.

**Inseam:** Measure from the crotch down the inside of the leg to the bottom of the ankle.

**Thigh:** Measure the circumference of the fullest part of the leg above the knee.

**Upper arm:** Measure the circumference of the widest part of the arm above the elbow.

**Sleeve length:** With a hand resting at the waist, start measuring from the middle of the back of the neck, across the shoulder, down the upper arm to the elbow, and then down to the wrist.

A short-waisted figure appears to have a top half that's proportionally smaller than the bottom half. A short-waisted girl can lengthen her appearance by wearing a top with vertical lines, tops that can be left untucked, and avoiding dresses with waistbands. The key here is to avoid drawing attention to the waistline.

The legs appear short in proportion to the top of a long-waisted figure. This figure can be enhanced by an A-line or empire waist dress, shirts that cover the waist, pants that sit at the natural waistline or a bit above, short jackets, high heeled shoes, and monochromatic shoes, hosiery, and skirts.

Regardless of body type, a monochromatic look (all the same color) tends to elongate the body's appearance.

Off-the-shoulder tops with full, flowing sleeves can mask thick upper arms. Scarves, turtleneck sweaters, cowls, and high collars can conceal a long neck. Unbuttoning the top button of a shirt or wearing a shirt with a V-neck can elongate the appearance of a short neck.

The famous "little black dress" that has become a wardrobe staple for women in most Western countries originated in the 1920s. It is credited to haute couture designers Coco Chanel and Jean Patou.

## DID YOU KNOW?

HIGH HEELS WERE FIRST USED IN THE NINTH CENTURY BY PERSIAN CAVALRY TO KEEP THEIR FEET FROM SLIDING THROUGH STIRRUPS.

# DETERMINING PERSONAL STYLE

Style can be categorized into a handful of basic groups. Before deciding her style, a girl should ask herself some personality-based questions:

- What are you most comfortable in?
- When not at school, what do you most like yourself in?
- What are your favorite accessories?
- What shoes do you prefer to wear most often?
- What colors do you prefer to wear?

The answers to these questions will help determine a girl's personal style. A few popular style categories include the following:

BOHEMIAN: Think hippie flower child. This girl likes to wear loose, flowing, romantic tops, skirts, and dresses in relaxed and casual, yet pretty styles. Her preferred color palette includes lots of white with earth tones with natural colors like turquoise, and coral.

PREPPY: This girl feels most comfortable in polo shirts, crisp pants or shorts, and cable knit sweaters. She prefers navy blue, kelly green, and pink; bold prints, argyles, and plaids; and crisp white or khaki.

URBAN: This type of girl goes for the sophisticated, big city style of New York, London, or Paris. She favors black accented with trendy colors.

CLASSIC: Girls who tend toward this look favor basic styles and colors that never go out of style, denim, white, and neutrals like black, gray, and beige. They add color through accessories.

Obviously, these categories generalize the many variations and individual tastes. One girl need not identify with a particular category and then shun everything favored by girls in other categories. These categories serve as guidelines upon which any girl can build her personal style.

# Sizes, Fibers, and Fabrics

**O**nce a girl has grown beyond the children's department, clothing sizes turn confusing. Unlike men's clothing, which is helpfully sized by neck and sleeve measurements (shirts) or waist and inseam measurements (pants), girls must make do with imprecise sizing that varies by manufacturer. A pair of pants in size 6 by one maker will most likely not be the same size as a size 6 by another label. Generally, cheaper clothing will be sized smaller than more expensive brands, and the upscale brands will feature more generous seam allowances to facilitate alteration for a custom fit. It is a good idea for young women to try on clothes before buying them to ensure (1) proper fit and (2) whether it looks good on her.

# CLOTHING SIZES

In the United States, clothing sizes for girls and women come in the following variations:

Misses—Even-numbered sizes made for the woman of an average height of 5 feet, 5 inches. Girls who run tall should seek out those clothiers that recognize women come in different heights and distinguish their clothes with short, average, and long lengths to accommodate lengthier legs and arms.

Juniors—Feminine clothing in odd-numbered sizes from 0 to 13 may be found in the "Juniors" section of a department store. Clothing in the Juniors section tends to run along trendier, more youthful styles and are primarily targeted to teenage girls.

Petite—Girls and women who are shorter than the average height of 5 feet, 5 inches often get an entire clothing section devoted to their proportionately smaller bodies and limbs.

Plus—Girls and women whose clothing runs larger than a Misses 14 will find apparel in the plus sizes, which run from 16 to extra-extra-extra-large (XXXL) sizes.

# FIBERS AND FABRICS

Bulky, shiny, or stiff fabrics add size. A pear-shaped girl who wants to add substance to her upper body might wear a thick, cable knit sweater. Soft,

# DRESSING ROOM ETIQUETTE

**M**ost clothing stores and even many discount stores provide dressing rooms to allow shoppers to try on clothes so they can assess fit and appearance. Many such stores have rules limiting the number of items that may be brought into the dressing rooms. It is polite to observe those rules.

When one has finished trying on a garment, place it back on the hanger if it was originally on a hanger. If not, then fold it neatly. Place the unwanted items on the rack designated for them to be returned to their proper locations by store personnel, if there is one, or return them to the proper clothing racks yourself. Store personnel are not maids employed to clean up after inconsiderate and messy shoppers. It's also impolite to leave a mess in the dressing room for the next shopper.

When it comes to panties and swimwear, it's polite and hygienic to observe lingerie fitting etiquette. In other words, wear panties when trying on panties or swimwear (including bikini bottoms). How many other girls have tried that on? There's no way to know. Just the idea of multiple fittings on multiple bodies ought to mandate that a girl protect her most vulnerable parts.

A farmer shears an alpaca for its wool. Alpaca and llama wool fibers are hollow core, making them more lightweight and warmer than sheep's wool.

drapey fabrics smooth bumps and rolls and flatter most body shapes. An apple-shaped girl looking to diminish her waistline should avoid wearing skin-tight, shiny fabric around her middle.

All clothes are made from fabric, which may be comprised of natural, manmade, or a blend of natural and manmade fibers. Until 1935, when DuPont invented nylon, all fabric was made from natural fibers. Excluding leather, which is the treated skin of an animal, the fibers that make fabric originate from a variety of sources and have varying properties. Oftentimes fibers are mixed together to take advantage of the strengths of each. Clothing purchased at retail stores has labels that list the fiber content, which help the shopper to make a decision about whether to purchase the garment.

Common natural fibers that come from plants include cotton, linen, and hemp. Natural fiber harvested from animals includes silk and wool. Silk comes from the cocoons of silkworms. Common wool may come from sheep, goats (mohair, cashmere), alpaca, and angora (rabbit). Those concerned with animal welfare should understand that harvesting wool does not require slaughter of the animal, unlike leather. Natural fibers often wrinkle easily. They are generally considered more comfortable to wear than manmade material and allow skin to breathe. Wool wicks moisture away; cotton absorbs moisture. Natural fabrics often shrink when washed in hot water and dried

Cotton, popular for its durability, softness, and comfort, is the best-selling fabric in the United States. The US ranks third globally when it comes to cotton production, after China and India.

on high heat, so care is needed in laundering.

Manmade fibers include acetate and rayon (made from wood pulp), nylon, acrylic, and polyester. The latter three are synthetic, meaning no plant or animal mat-

The various types of fiber can come in a variety of textures and colors.

ter is used in the manufacture. Because manmade fabric generally isn't as comfortable to wear as natural fabrics, manmade fiber is often blended with natural fiber to create fabrics that resist staining, have a little bit of stretch to them, and don't wrinkle as readily. Polyester, for instance, is often blended with cotton or wool to add strength and durability.

While natural fabrics might scorch or burn under a hot iron, synthetic fabrics will melt.

## WHAT COLOR WORKS BEST?

Once a girl has tried on enough clothing styles to determine what flatters her the most, it's finally time to focus on color. Despite the dictates of fashion designers, not every girl looks good in the season's trendiest colors.

Colors—whether light or dark or neutral—come in warm and cool tones. Warm colors have undertones of yellow, peach, or gold; cool colors have undertones of pink, red, or blue. The proper colors with the correct undertones will flatter a girl's complexion and hair. Undertones can be used to harmonize colors in an outfit—or in décor—and to emphasize or downplay elements. To determine whether one's skin has cool or warm undertones:

1) Check your veins. If the veins on the inside of the wrist are bluish, then you likely have cool undertones. Greenish veins indicate warm undertones.

2) Try jewelry. Does gold or silver look better against your skin? Silver and platinum look better on girls with cool undertones; gold looks better on skin with warm undertones.

3) Look at neutral colors. Cool-toned skin will look better in black or white, which makes warm-toned skin look sallow. Ivory, brown, and beige look better against warm-toned skin, which can make cool-toned skin look washed-out.

4) Get some sun. Skin that's more likely to tan than burn generally fits into the category of having warm undertones. Skin that's more likely to turn pink and burn before tanning generally has cool undertones.

Different seasons and occasions lend themselves to color categories. Pastels come out in the spring; bright colors signal the arrival of summer; darker, richer colors herald autumn; and jewel tones take fashion into winter. Somber and serious occasions call for dark and neutral colors.

# Build on the Existing Wardrobe

**F**ashion isn't about looking trendy—fashion is about looking good. Basic education and experimentation in fabric, body shape, and color will go a long way toward building a style that fits a girl's personality and budget.

Fashion experts know the trick of building a fashionable wardrobe around a core set of key pieces. Even girls who are still growing can take advantage of this tactic to build their wardrobes. Before heading off on a shopping trip, inventory your wardrobe.

## WARDROBE TRIAGE

Sort your clothes into four categories:

**Favorites:** These are clothes in good condition that fit well, look good, and which will definitely be worn.

**Keepers:** These are clothes that fit, but don't inspire strongly negative or positive feelings. They're just okay and will probably be worn.

**Discard:** These are clothes that you have outgrown, are in poor condition, are just plain ugly, or are hopelessly outdated. They won't be worn and they're not useful as hand-me-downs to younger siblings.

**Donation:** These are clothes that are in good condition, but have been outgrown or just don't look good. They can be donated to charity or handed down to younger siblings.

Put the garments from the "favorites" and "keepers" categories back in your closet and/or bureau. These will serve as the core around which the new wardrobe will be built. Glamour magazine and other fashion sources expand the list of wardrobe staples from Chapter 2 to include other specific items that a grown woman would wear, such as the ubiquitous little black dress and a trench coat. The key is to remember that inexpensive does not have to look cheap.

The first rule of fashion is to wear clothes that fit properly. A girl who has a close relative or friend who sews can ask for assistance in having that person help to alter her favorite pieces and, perhaps, teach her how to do it herself. Needles, thread, and a good pair of scissors aren't that expensive and enable the thrifty girl to turn baggy, ill-fitting clothing into something flattering.

Thrift stores or secondhand stores are great places to find vintage or good-quality clothing at affordable prices.

# FRUGAL, IMPRESSIVE IMPROVEMENTS

Many small alterations don't require expert knowledge of sewing, but can make an impressive difference in the appearance of a girl's wardrobe.

REPLACE BUTTONS: You can update coats, blouses, jackets—anything with buttons—by replacing the cheap, plastic buttons that came with the garment with new buttons made of metal, ceramic, bone, or fabric-covered plastic. You might even be able to scavenge buttons off a discarded coat that an older sibling or relative no longer wears. Be sure to use a thread of the same color or just a tiny shade darker than the fabric of garment.

A girl might even want to experiment with replacing buttons with frog fasteners. Sometimes referred to as a Chinese frog, this fastener is created from ornamental braiding consisting of a button-and-loop closure that is sewn on the outside surface of the garment, serving dual purposes of fastener and decoration. They're commonly used on tops with Mandarin collars and on military style jackets. Frog fasteners can be purchased ready to sew onto the garment and are available from any fabric store, many craft stores, and online sources like Etsy and Amazon. They come in many colors.

Replacing plastic buttons with fancier metal ones is an inexpensive way to dress up a coat or other garment.

IRON WRINKLED CLOTHING: If you have access to a steamer, it can be used to remove the wrinkles from heavy garments like winter coats and blazers.

Lighter weight items should be ironed. Use the temperature guides on the iron and the care instructions on the garment to ensure the iron is heated to the proper temperature. Synthetic fabrics will melt if the iron's temperature is set too high. Natural fibers may scorch if a hot iron is pressed against the fabric for too long. Learn which fabrics are predisposed to wrinkling. Well-pressed clothing looks crisp and well cared for; wrinkly clothing cheapens the look.

Ironing clothes isn't "women's" work—learning how to iron is a skill that every adult will find useful.

**GET A FABRIC SHAVER:** Nothing else makes a sweater look tired, worn, and cheap more than pills, those little fuzzballs that collect on the surface of the knit. If you pull them, you run the risk of snagging the threads. Cutting them off with a scissors might inadvertently snip a thread that will begin to unravel and create an unsightly hole in the sweater. A fabric shaver removes the pills from the garment and leaves the surface looking like new. They run from about $6 to $20, and can be found in discount stores like Target or Walmart, as well as in drugstores like Walgreens.

**TAKE CARE OF YOUR SHOES:** Especially for older teens whose feet have stopped growing, judicious use of shoe polish and a buffing cloth can cover scratches in leather shoes and help make shoes look practically new. Those who have access to a shoe repair shop can take their best shoes in to have worn heels and soles replaced. Treated with care, shoes will last longer and look better. Also, if you have lots of white leather shoes and little in the way of other colors, shoe polish can be used to recolor your shoes. This can

## TIPS TO DYE FOR

Start with clean fabric, so be sure the garment is freshly laundered. Dye may stain the container that you're using, so use a clean bucket or something that parents won't mind if it gets stained. Put down a drop cloth to protect the floor around the container full of dye.

Martha Stewart recommends adding some white vinegar if dying wool or silk, or adding salt when dying cotton or linen. The additives will help the color set.

After dying the fabric, rinse it in running water until the water runs clear. Be sure to rinse out the bucket or sink immediately, too.

It's not necessary to invest in expensive fabric dyes; several items that can be found around the average family home can be used to dye cloth. Fans of tan, beige, brown, or ecru can dye fabric using tea or coffee. For other colors, use Kool-Aid, which can impart surprisingly vivid colors.

be less expensive than buying new ones. Shoe polish kits can be found in any big box department store or even the supermarket.

Dye fabric for a whole new look. Rather than buy a new shirt in the latest trendy color, take an old white or light-colored shirt and dye it to give it new life. It might just become a favorite piece again. Understand that natural fabrics take dye better than synthetics, and that different dyes work differently. Trim and stitching may also take dye differently from the fabric, so follow instructions carefully.

Five thousand years ago, buttons were first used as ornaments and seals, not as fasteners. Not until the 1200s were buttons used to fasten clothing. This dragon carved from ivory was a fastener on a Japanese kimono, circa 1700.

The zipper, originally called a clasp locker, was invented in Chicago by Whitcomb L. Judson in 1893. Zippers did not come into widespread use on garments until the 1910s.

# Fashion Through Accessories

Fashion gurus emphasize the versatility and impact of well-chosen accessories. From handbags to scarves to belts to jewelry, accessories can add color and texture, as well as draw attention to specific areas and away from other areas. Accessories can be expensive, though, so choose wisely and focus on acquiring good quality items that will last a long time.

## HANDBAGS

Simplify the handbag. Any girl who carries a purse may be tempted to get one with lots of fancy buckles and snapped pockets and other embellishments. Don't be distracted. One simple handbag that's well made will coordinate better with more of your wardrobe than will a bunch of cheaply made bags. It will last longer, too. Signs of a well-made purse include:

- fabric lining
- neat, small stitching at the seams

- secure attachment of all hardware (zippers, snaps, buttons, etc.)
- substantial straps that won't easily break and can be adjusted to fit. (You may need to lengthen shoulder straps when carrying your purse over bulky winter clothes to comfortably accommodate the extra fabric of sweater and coat.)

Consider the size of your handbag. It's not a backpack and it's not meant to carry school textbooks and homework. A purse that is too large can overwhelm a girl's outfit. The shape of the purse should complement her figure. A rule of thumb is that body shape and purse shape should not match. Tall girls look best with large, unstructured shoulder bags, cross-body messenger bags, trapezoid or ruffled satchels, or handheld clutches. Hobo, baguettes with straps, bucket bags, and small briefcases look best with petite girls. Curvy bodies look best with structured, framed bags.

A tall girl can rock a larger handbag or shoulder bag.

Like any accessory, it's important to try on purses like you try on clothes, and to pick a handbag that will at least hold the essentials (wallet, small pack of tissues, keys, comb, lip gloss, cell phone, maxi pads or tampons, etc.), and maybe a paperback book. The purse should be held (by handle or shoulder strap) either above or below the waist.

Some handbags can be laundered. Before throwing a dirty purse into the wash, check for elements that are not machine washable. If you're not sure, ask an adult or consult the manufacturer's website. Washable handbags are usually made of cotton or even wool, although some may be made of manmade materials. Before buying a fabric purse, make sure the cloth is sturdy and tightly woven so it doesn't snag and will hold up to the rigors of daily use.

Leather purses may be wiped down with a damp cloth and some mild cleaner specifically formulated for leather. Saddle soap works well. Follow the instructions on the cleaning product.

Velvet, linen, or suede purses must be dry cleaned. Girls on a tight budget may wish to steer clear of purses that will need dry cleaning to keep looking good.

When choosing a purse, consider security. While it's convenient to simply reach into a huge, open pocket to retrieve a desired item, others can do the same. Flaps that snap shut and zippers help prevent others from helping themselves to the contents of your purse. A good closure will also prevent items from spilling out of the purse if it should be dropped.

One big pocket or lots of little pockets? Everyone has her preferences, so get what best suits you. Regardless, every good purse needs one or two small, discreet pockets that zip closed to contain and conceal very personal items.

# WEAR A SLIP

Yes, it's old-fashioned. But slips do serve a necessary purpose. First, they help a girl's dresses and skirts flow more smoothly over her body and conceal those unsightly lines created by tight bra straps and panties. Second, they protect her skin from rough or itchy fabrics. Third, they help maintain her modesty, especially when she doesn't want people to see through her clothing.

Slips come in two basic designs: full and half. A full slip covers the body from shoulders to knees. A girl usually wears a full slip with a dress.

# MAKE SURE UNDERGARMENTS FIT PROPERLY

A dolescent girls learn a dramatic lesson that adults sometimes forget: their body shapes can change. A girl who's well developed enough to wear a bra needs to know how one should fit properly. A poorly fitted bra is not only uncomfortable, it creates ugly bulges and rolls that show beneath her clothing.

There are two ways to determine bra size. FIrst, bring a measuring tape around the back and under the arms and across the middle of your chest. Write down that number. If the number is odd, then make a note to round up to the next even number. The next measurement is the circumference of the torso directly under the breasts for the bottom of the band. As before, an odd number should be rounded up to the next even number.

Measuring cup size gets tricky. Bring the measuring tape loosely around at the fullest part of the bust. Subtract the band measurement from the bust measurement. Each inch in difference represents a cup size: 1 inch is an A cup, 2 inches a B cup, 3 inches a C cup, 4 inches a D cup, and so on.

With these measurements in mind, it's time to try on bras. Yes, in order to ensure a proper fit, one must try them on, especially since breasts come in different shapes as well as different sizes. Different brands of bras fit differently, and

Shoulders should have adjustable straps to customize the fit. Sizes vary, with adult sizes based on corresponding dress and bust sizes. A chemise is a shorter version of a full slip and serve well under dresses with hems that rise above the knee. A chemise usually features some extra ornamenta-

some brands will accommodate an individual girl's shape better than others. Be aware that the center piece (panel) between the bra cups should rest flat against the breastbone (sternum). Padding, underwires, and panel width and depth all affect the fit of a bra.

When it comes to panties, comfort is important. Thongs may be fashionable, but don't feel pressured to force yourself into something you don't find comfortable. A properly fitting pair of panties doesn't sag or bag, especially between the legs. Neither do they dig or pinch into the waist or hips or elsewhere. Panties that fit well will have a crotch that has no excess fabric drooping down. Synthetic materials, like nylon, can feel itchy since they don't breathe well. Natural fibers breathe. Cotton panties breathe best and are recommended for sensitive skin, especially for young women who are prone to yeast infections. If the seams chafe or the elastic around the legs pinches, then the panties will be uncomfortable. Don't buy them. Seamless panties help reduce panty lines and may even prevent yeast infections.

One last word on panties: a girl should learn which styles she likes to wear: Briefs, hip huggers, bikini, thongs, G-string, etc. Some girls find thongs and G-strings comfortable, others don't. Be aware that your panties preference may change at certain times of the month, particularly if you use maxi pads instead of tampons.

tion, like lots of lace. Half-slips cover from the waist down and are usually worn with skirts. They can be paired with camisoles for full coverage under a dress.

This inexpensive undergarment, usually made of nylon for year-round use or cotton for summertime, usually comes in three colors: nude, black, and white. It's best to go with a neutral color that won't show through one's clothing. Find a slip in the intimate apparel section of your local department store.

# JEWELRY

Add sparkle with jewelry. Most girls depend upon parents and relatives to buy them jewelry or may be content to borrow from their mothers' and older sisters' jewelry boxes. However, a girl who wants to buy her own jewelry is well advised to save her money until she can invest in a quality piece.

This doesn't mean she has to invest in solid gold and diamonds; it does mean that a few, well-crafted pieces made of quality materials will look better and last longer than cheap jewelry with a finish that tarnishes quickly, flakes away, or turns her skin green. Good quality costume jewelry will spruce up your look at an affordable cost.

Essential pieces of jewelry include: a pearl necklace and stud earrings, diamond or cubic zirconia stud earrings, and a simple pendant necklace (gold or silver). Girls seeking pieces to last them into adulthood should avoid trendy velvet necklaces, dog collar chokers, heavily beaded chokers, and ribbon or string-tied necklaces. A statement brooch can add a splash

The name "costume jewelry" originated in the 1920s to describe inexpensive ornamental necklaces, earrings, or bracelets worn to accentuate a particular outfit (or "costume").

of color or sparkle to an otherwise dull outfit.

Sterling silver can often be found at inexpensive prices, especially when not accompanied by real gemstones. Silver by itself has a soft gleam that complements nearly every skin tone. If you really want to add sparkle, don't dismiss rhinestones. At a casual glance, rhinestones can't be distinguished from the real thing and look just as pretty for a fraction of the price.

Another inexpensive way to add to your selection of jewelry is to shop garage sales and thrift stores. You'll find old pieces that were once worn by someone's grandmother, which can be polished and cleaned and restored to beauty.

# SCARVES

Add colorful pizzazz with scarves. Scarves come in a variety of sizes, textures, and fabrics. Their myriad uses transform them from simple rectangles of fabric to garments of clothing to eye-catching fashion accessories that make an outfit look chic and stylish. Scarves can add much-needed color to neutral colors, draw attention away from certain body parts, and conceal other body parts to assist in achieving a balanced appearance. Those who are not sure what to do with a scarf or how to tie one can find a plethora of options demonstrated on YouTube or other internet sites.

A colorful scarf can dress up even the simplest outfit.

A pashmina is a colorful scarf made from a special wool grown in Central Asia.

# Shopping Suggestions

**A**ccording to the *Kansas City Star*, the National Retail Federation surveyed shoppers and learned that the average family spends $673.57 per year on back-to-school clothing purchases. RetailMeNot Inc. conducted two surveys to find that parents spent an average of $273 on each child's back-to-school clothing. If you don't have more than $1,000 to spend on a year's worth of clothing, invest your limited funds in a few signature pieces.

Fashions change with every season. What was in style last spring won't be in style next spring, and no girl wants to look hopelessly out of fashion. Even with a few well-chosen pieces, she wants to show her friends and rivals that she can be in style or even set the style. For a girl on a limited budget, it's time to get creative.

# What's Old Is New Again

Fashion designers often look back to past decades for inspiration. Recent trends in girls' fashion draw from the exuberance of the 1970s: bell bottom pants, flowery prints, peasant blouses, flowing lines. Mother or grand-mothers who haven't thrown out their clothes from their youth may have wonderful resources a girl can dig through. Thrift stores offer other great, low-cost options for satisfying that desire to comply with fashion trends. Bargain seekers can find practically brand new and lightly used clothing, often upscale brands, at low, low prices.

For clothing styles that harken back fifty years or more ago, look for shops that sell vintage clothing. Adding the word "vintage" raises the price, but savvy shoppers can still find good deals that spruce up their wardrobes and help them establish great looking styles.

# Prints, Patterns and Shoes

Price, cut, and style are all important. However, other factors also affect fashion. Some have specific seasonal associations, while others are appropriate for year-round wear.

**Denim.** A girl can't go wrong with denim. Since the 1970s, denim has become a wardrobe staple. It's durable, comfortable, works across all four seasons, and goes with almost anything.

**Leather.** Not exactly the favorite material for hot weather wear, leather offers richness and durability and texture to a wardrobe. A bomber jacket with shearling collar, suede skirt, knee-high equestrian boots, and other signature pieces might be pricey, but just one or two pieces will add substance to a girl's wardrobe, especially paired with seasonally appropriate pieces.

**Prints.** Floral prints can brighten up a wardrobe and are especially appropriate in spring and summer. Prints can be subtle, tone-on-tone or attention-grabbing bright. Prints allow for mixing of colors that one might not ordinarily wear together.

**Plaids.** A staple of cold weather clothing, wool plaids evoke the misty reaches of Scotland and Ireland, kilts, and hot cups of tea by the fire. The trick to wearing plaid is to find a pattern that doesn't overwhelm. A plaid skirt or jacket looks best when paired with solid colored coordinates.

Leather jackets require special care to remain pliable and looking good. When properly cared for, items made from leather or fur can last for up to twenty years.

# FOOTWEAR TIPS

Girls can't go wrong obeying the traditional fashion rule of wearing white shoes only between Memorial Day and Labor Day. Brown, tan, black, taupe, and gray footwear is appropriate for the rest of the year. Every girl should have one pair each of dress shoes, casual shoes, sandals, and boots.

# Fashion Faux Pas

No book on fashion is complete without a cautionary statement about those errors that destroy a girl's style. Fashion experts cringe when they see:

- Visible panties above the waistline of one's skirt or pants. Panties should remain unseen.

- Wedding guests who wear white, ivory, or ecru. Only the bride should wear white, ivory, or ecru.

- Bare midriffs. Even if a girl has a fabulously toned body, a naked belly is too casual for anything except the beach.

- Pantyhose with open-toed shoes. If it's warm enough to wear sandals, then it's too warm for stockings. If it's cool enough for stockings, then it's too cool for sandals.

- Pants that are too short. Capris aside, "high water" pants or "floods" reduce the appearance of the length of one's legs.

- White undergarments under anything sheer. Undergarments not only provide support, but they protect one's modesty. White undergarments draw attention to what they're covering. Opt instead for nude or flesh-toned undergarments beneath sheer clothing.

- Bra straps that show. Bra straps on display just cheapen a girl's look and draw attention to her undergarments, not her style.

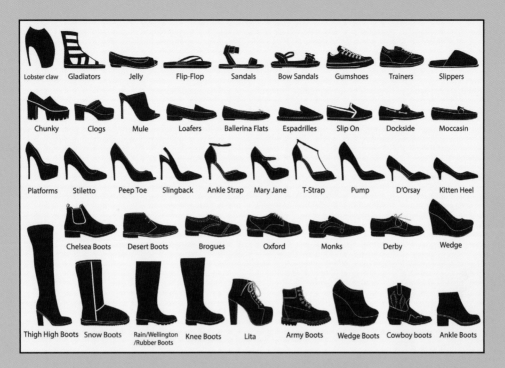

Shoes carry a language all their own. They have their own parts. The vamp is the part of the shoe that covers the top of the foot. The sole is the bottom of the shoe. The counter is the back of the shoe. The heel supports the back of the foot and determines the height of the shoe.

Pumps are shoes that cover the toe box, have a high or low heel, and slip on without a fastening (shoelaces, buckles, etc.). Mules are basically pumps without a counter. Sandals come in a variety of styles. Sneakers and sport shoes can be very specialized to a particular sport or simply casual footwear. Boots, usually leather, range from shafts that extend over the knee to just around the ankle and vary in heel height. Other styles abound. Except for boots, which are usually leather, footwear comes in a variety of materials, from cheap plastic to leather to canvas to faille (a silky fabric) to dressy satin.

# COLD WEATHER COMMON SENSE

In many places, winter means frigid temperatures that can turn lethal for the inappropriately dressed person. Winter outerwear is not an area to skimp on quality. Cold weather gear, however, does not mean that a girl must look like a troll. Even snow boots can be stylish and paired with the right outfit and a coat that flatters a girl's shape.

Freezing weather means adding material bulk to a girl's silhouette. Experts recommend layering clothes first for warmth, then for fashion. Tank tops, tee shirts, and button-down shirts can be layered under cardigan sweaters. A silk undershirt beneath a thin sweater can add warmth without adding a lot of bulk. Natural fibers are preferred over manmade fibers, with the exception of cotton, for winter wear.

When considering a winter coat, fashion experts recommend the classic trench coat or peacoat. Those never go out of style and should never be worn unbuttoned.

Cotton absorbs moisture and clings to skin, leaving skin damp with perspiration. Damp skin chills faster and is more highly prone to frostbite than dry skin. Wool and silk do not readily absorb moisture, which means they draw moisture away from the surface of the skin and maintain loft. Loft helps to hold a layer of warm air against the skin, which protects against cold. Dry skin stays warmer longer and is more comfortable. Wool and silk also insulate better than cotton.

Cold weather wisdom advises wearing wool socks, hats, scarves, and gloves or mittens. Be aware that wool, although more expensive, is warmer than manmade fibers. Take the climate and the activity into consideration when buying cold weather gear.

# SEW IT

The final word about fashion on a budget concerns sewing one's own clothes. Any girl (or boy) who embarks upon this adventure must first understand that sewing is a skill that takes time and practice to refine. Early attempts will likely result in garments not fit for public viewing.

Sewing, however, offers not only a useful skill but also a creative outlet. Girls who learn to sew well can not only alter their own clothes, they can also create their own outfits, and possibly even design new styles for themselves. Home economics classes often include a few weeks on basic sewing skills. Relatives can often be called upon for instruction. Fabric stores and craft shops may offer sewing classes in addition to all the necessary sewing supplies.

Any girl hesitant about learning to sew should remember this: every prominent fashion designer knows how to sew. Donna Karan, Karl Lagerfeld, Tom Ford, Calvin Klein, Vera Wang—they all sew. That's how they construct their design prototypes to figure out what works and what doesn't. Before you consign the handy skill of sewing to the musty past, consider how useful that skill could be in enabling you to save money by enabling you to customize key pieces of clothing to last longer.

# Glossary

**bustle**—a framework that expands the fullness or supports the drapery of the back of a woman's dress.

**circumference**—the enclosing boundary of a curved figure.

**corset**—a constricting garment that covers the body from breast to hip. It is traditionally worn to reshape the torso in accordance with fashion trends.

**crinoline**—a stiffened or structured petticoat that holds skirts away from the wearer's legs, often used to effect a fashionable silhouette.

**etiquette**—a customary code for polite behavior.

**felled seam**—also called flat-fell seam, is a seam made by placing one edge of fabric inside a folded edge of fabric and then stitching the fold down.

**frugal**—sparing or economical.

**hoop skirt**—a woman's undergarment incorporating a fabric petticoat sewn with channels through which whalebone, steel, or other stiffening agents were threaded to expand the silhouette below the waist and even to stay cooler in hot climates.

**measuring tape**—a flexible ruler consisting of a ribbon of cloth or plastic with linear measurement markings.

**seam allowance**—also called inlays, this is the area between the edge of the fabric and the line of stitching (seam) connecting two or more pieces of fabric.

**triage**—the process of determining priority or importance, usually used in the medical field to determine which patients receive treatment first.

# Types of Fabric Often Used for Clothing

**boucle**—plain or twill weave made from looped yarns that give it a textured, nubby surface.

**broadcloth**—fine, tightly woven fabric with a slight horizontal rib.

**brocade**—a heavy, decorative cloth characterized by raised designs woven into the material, often used for furniture upholstery.

**calico**—plain-weave cloth with small, often colored, motifs.

**cashmere**—soft, warm cloth woven from the wool of a cashmere goat.

**chantilly lace**—lightweight, sheer, airy fabric with highly twisted fibers.

**corduroy**—cotton or cotton blend fabric with a cut-pile weave. The number of cords per inch is called the wale.

**crepe**—fabric with a crinkled, crimped, or grainy surface.

**dobby**—decorative weave with small patterns that are usually geometric.

**duck**—closely woven, plain or ribbed cotton, more lightweight than canvas and often used for furniture upholstery or jackets.

**faille**—closely knit, heavy, glossy fabric with flat, crosswise ribs.

**gabardine**—twill weave, worsted fabric.

**gingham**—plain weave fabric with a checkerboard pattern, usually white and another color.

**herringbone**—twill weave with a zigzag effect.

**microfiber**—fine synthetic fabric noted for being durable, washable, breathable, and water repellent, often used for furniture upholstery.

**satin**—smooth, shiny fabric.

**spandex**—stretchy fabric, also known as Lycra.

**taffeta**—crisp, tightly woven fabric often with a subtle sheen and famous for its rustling sound.

# Further Reading

Brescia, George. *Change Your Clothes, Change Your Life*. New York: Gallery Books, 2014.

Goodman, Amy. *Wear This, Toss That!: Hundreds of Fashion and Beauty Swaps that Save Your Looks, Save Your Budget and Save Your Time*. New York: Simon and Schuster, 2011.

Low, Rachel. *Girl's Guide to DIY Fashion: Design and Sew 5 Complete Outfits*. Lafayette, Calif: CandT Publishing, 2015.

Martin, Jill, and Pierre Lehu, with Dana Ravich. *Fashion for Dummies*. Hoboken, NJ: Wiley Publishing, 2010.

Thompson, Henrietta. *Remake It: Clothes*. London: Thames and Hudson, 2012.

Wild, Denise. *Mend and Make Fabulous: Sewing Solutions and Fashionable Fixes*. Loveland, Colo.: Interweave, 2014.

Zarian, Lawrence. *10 Commandments for a Perfect Wardrobe*. Los Angeles: Bird Street Books, 2014.

# Internet Resources

http://www.whowhatwear.com/budget-cheap-style-tips-fashion-winter-2014.
   "11 Style Tips for the Girl on a Shoestring Budget" by Kat Collings. Published by
   WhoWhatWear, February 19, 2014.

http://www.ebay.com/gds/7-Important-Features-of-a-Handbag-
/10000000177742812/g.html
   This article details the features of a quality handbag.

http://www.ebay.com/gds/How-to-Choose-the-Right-Slip-for-Your-Dress-
/10000000177631023/g.html
   This article offers advice on styles, fabrics, and materials in slips.

http://www.marthastewart.com/1110589/fit-be-dyed
   This domestic maven offers clear instructions on how to dye fabric.

http://jseverydayfashion.com/home/2012/08/how-to-not-look-cheap.html
   This blog addresses fashion concerns for women of all ages.

http://www.barenecessities.com/feature.aspx?pagename=fit_sizing
   This article addresses how to fit a bra.

http://www.seventeen.com/fashion/style-advice/g2849/denim-myths-rules/?
   Longstanding beauty and fashion magazine for teenage girls.

http://www.glamour.com/gallery/wardrobe-staples-essential-fashion-and-
clothing-items#1
   Longstanding fashion and beauty magazine for women.

# Index

Numbers in **bold italic** refer to captions.